G000098057

Emergent
Dictionary

Ginny Lapage
Illustrated by James Dunbar

Introduction

This is the first dictionary in a series of three for Emergent, Early and Independent readers. It has been devised with the active help of the children and teachers of a primary school who were involved at all the stages of compilation.

The series of dictionaries have been designed to lead children in stages into using more formal dictionaries. They are intended to be fun as well as to give information.

This Emergent Dictionary has been designed to introduce dictionary skills to children who are at the earliest stages of reading. It is presented as the first small step towards using an adult dictionary and so it is arranged in alphabetical order rather than by topic. The 177 words are all nouns with the definitions shown as full-colour illustrations. (Only the singular form of the spelling is given.) A full alphabet is printed at the bottom of each page with the appropriate letter highlighted in colour.

Ginny Lapage is an experienced primary school teacher. She has an M.A. in Children's Literature and a Diploma in reading and Language Development. She has compiled the *Collins Junior Dictionary*, the accompanying workbook and the workbooks for *Collins Picture Dictionary* and *Collins Primary Dictionary*.

a b c d e f g h i j k l m

How to use this dictionary

The main aim of this book is to give enjoyment. Children should be encouraged to talk about the pictures as they look through the book and gradually they will be able to match the words to the pictures and begin to recognise individual words. As children become familiar with the alphabet, they will be able to pick out the first letter of the word and find it in the border at the bottom of the page.

Aa

aeroplane

a b c d e f g h i j k l m

Aa

ant

apple

baby

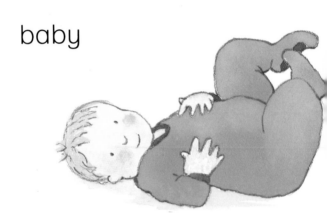

bag

a **b** c d e f g h i j k l m

ball

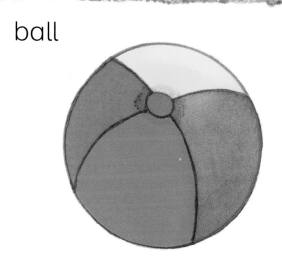

balloon

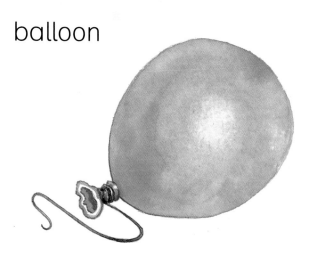

n o p q r s t u v w x y z   7

banana

basket

a **b** c d e f g h i j k l m

Bb

bat

beach

bean

bear

a **b** c d e f g h i j k l m

bed

bee

bike

bird

a **b** c d e f g h i j k l m

biscuit

book

boot

bottle

box

bread

broom

bus

cake

car

cat

chair

chest of drawers

clock

clothes

a b **c** d e f g h i j k l m

cloud

coat

Cc

cow

cup

a b **c** d e f g h i j k l m

cupboard

curtain

dinosaur

dish

a b c **d** e f g h i j k l m

Dd

dog

door

drum

duck

a b c **d** e f g h i j k l m

egg

eye

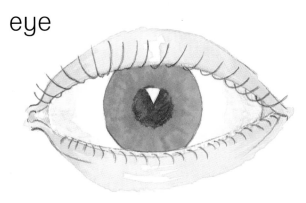

n o p q r s t u v w x y z   27

Ff

face

farm

a b c d e **f** g h i j k l m

farmer

feather

Ff

fence

field

a b c d e f g h i j k l m

finger

firefighter

Ff

fish

flower

fly

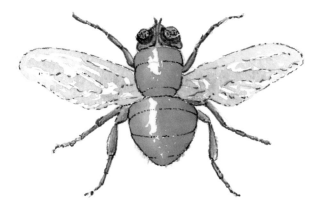

food

Ff

foot

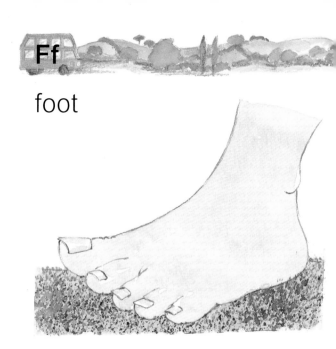

football

a b c d e **f** g h i j k l m

footprint

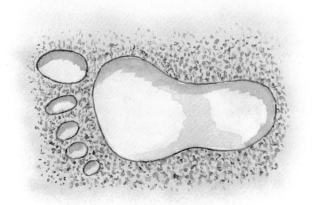

fox

Ff

frog

fruit

a b c d e **f** g h i j k l m

Gg

garden

giant

glove

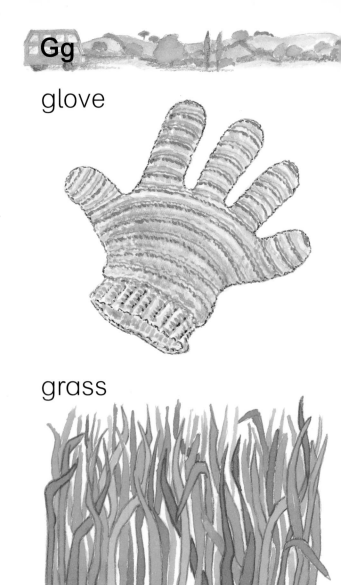

grass

a b c d e f **g h** i j k l m

hall

hat

hedgehog

hippopotamus

horse

housefly

ice

ice-cream

a b c d e f g h i j k l m

jacket

jam

jeans

jumble sale

 K k

kitchen

kitten

Ll

ladder

lake

a b c d e f g h i j k l m

lemonade

letter

2 King Street
Norwich
NR14AF
21 April
Dear Ben
Thank you
for the lovely
present.
Love
Polly

Ll

lion

litter

a b c d e f g h i j k **l** m

map

milk

mirror

monster

moon

mouse

nest

net

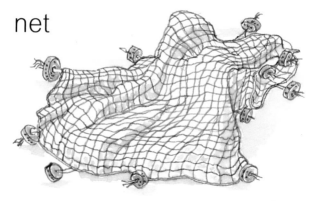

a b c d e f g h i j k l m

nose

nurse

Oo

orange

a b c d e f g h i j k l m

paper

park

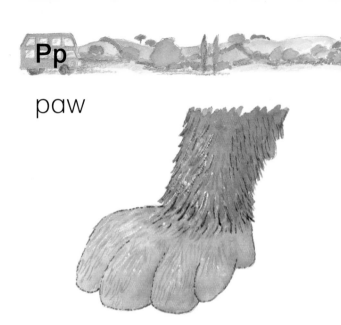

paw

pea

Pp

petal

petrol

picture

pig

a b c d e f g h i j k l m

pipe

pirate

plant

playground

a b c d e f g h i j k l m

pocket

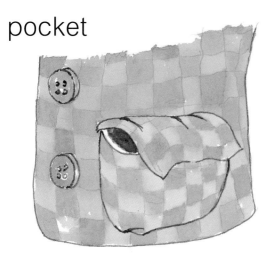

police car

pond

potato

present

puddle

puppy

pyjamas

queen

Rr

rat

a b c d e f g h i j k l m

river

road

Rr

robin

room

a b c d e f g h i j k l m

rope

roundabout

saucepan

scarecrow

school

scissors

Ss

sea

seal

a b c d e f g h i j k l m

seat

shed

sheep

sheepdog

a b c d e f g h i j k l m

shelf

shoe

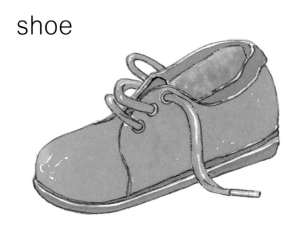

shop

skirt

a b c d e f g h i j k l m

Ss

sky

sleeve

snake

snow

a b c d e f g h i j k l m

sock

spider

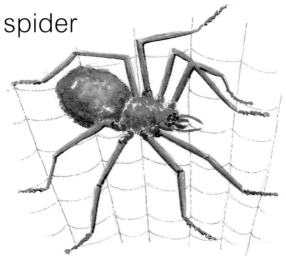

squirrel

stair

star

straw

street

sun

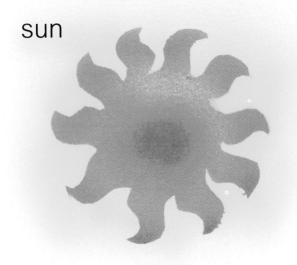

sweet

swing

table

a b c d e f g h i j k l m

tail

toad

toast

tongue

tooth

town

toy

tree

trousers

turtle

U u

uniform

V v

a b c d e f g h i j k l m

walrus

wand

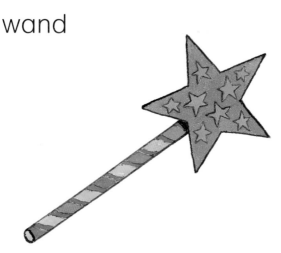

wardrobe

washing line

water

whale

window